AZORES TRAVEL GUIDE
2023

Discover Azores: An idea Tour Guide to the Hidden Gems of Azores: Explore the Natural Wonders, Cultural Attraction, Farming, local Cuisine with it's best 14 days Itinerary 2023

By

Charles B. Hogan

Table of Contents

My Azores Travel Experience

My recent trip to the Azores Islands was a wonderful experience! I had heard about the spectacular beauty of the Azores from friends and family who had gone before, but I was still amazed when I eventually arrived. The islands are located in the center of the Atlantic Ocean, and they are home to spectacular cliffs, lush woods, and stunning beaches.

The first thing that hit me when I arrived was the magnificent countryside. I was stunned by the sheer beauty of the islands, especially the lush green trees, rolling hills, and the glittering blue of the ocean. I felt so small and insignificant in the presence of such beauty and grandeur. I spent a lot of time just touring the different regions of the islands, and soaking up the natural beauty.

One of my favorite parts of the trip was visiting the hot springs. The Azores are home to several natural hot springs, and these were a genuine delight. The water was crystal clear and the temperature was ideal. I could feel my stress just melting away as I soaked in the natural healing waters.

I also really enjoyed seeing the local towns and villages. I was able to explore a very distinct culture, with the natives being so warm and hospitable. I loved researching their unique cuisine and tasting all the different meals.

The beaches were also something else. I loved spending time at the beach, resting in the sun, and swimming in the crystal blue waters. The beaches in the Azores are some of the most beautiful in the world, and I was so pleased to experience them for myself.

My journey to the Azores was one of the most unforgettable and beautiful experiences of my life. I was very astonished at the beauty of the islands and the wonderful welcome of the residents. I would recommend a visit to the Azores to anyone looking for a truly unique and unforgettable experience.

Introduction

The Azores, an archipelago of nine volcanic islands located off the coast of Portugal in the North Atlantic Ocean, is an autonomous area of Portugal and an increasingly famous tourist destination for people from all over the world.

The islands, which are spread out across an area of around 860 square kilometers, provide a unique combination of natural beauty, vibrant culture, and recreational activities. The archipelago is home to beautiful landscapes, from lush green slopes to craggy volcanic peaks, which have led to it being termed the "Hawaii of the Atlantic".

The islands are also recognized for their unique cultural legacy, with a combination of traditional

Portuguese and African elements. From colorful festivals to traditional food, the Azores offer a varied cultural experience for visitors. This is accompanied by a range of leisure activities, including whale viewing, surfing, and hiking.

The Azores are also recognized for their kind and inviting people, who are proud to share their culture and hospitality with visitors. The islanders are proud of their culture and history, and this is reflected in their commitment to conserving the islands' natural beauty and cultural heritage.

Due to their natural beauty and rich cultural heritage, the Azores are an increasingly popular tourist destination. With a multitude of activities and attractions, they provide something for everyone. Whether it's exploring the volcanic landscape, discovering the distinct culture, or simply relaxing on the beaches, the Azores are a fantastic vacation for tourists searching for an exceptional experience.

Brief History of Azores

The Azores, a group of nine volcanic islands, are located in the North Atlantic Ocean, roughly 1,500 km (930 mi) west of mainland Portugal. The islands have a rich history, with settlers arriving in the archipelago as early as the 15th century.

The first settlers of the Azores were the Portuguese, who came in the 15th century. The early settlers were largely farmers and fishermen, who found the islands to be a perfect area to raise crops and catch fish. The Portuguese were also able to take advantage of the island's strategic location, which made them a suitable layover spot for ships traveling between Europe and the Americas.

In the 16th century, the Azores became an important trading center for the Portuguese, and the islands prospered as a result. The archipelago was also a popular resting point for ships heading throughout the world, and many of the major European nations maintained a presence in the Azores.

In the 17th century, the islands were occupied by the Spaniards. This occupation continued until the 18th century when the Portuguese recovered control of the Azores.

The 19th century saw the islands become a major whaling hub, and the whaling business was an important component of the Azorean economy until the early 20th century. This period was also marked by the entry of new residents, particularly from the Portuguese mainland and Madeira.

The 20th century was a period of economic and political turmoil in the Azores. At this time, the islands experienced a period of rapid industrialization, which led to an inflow of immigrants from the mainland and other areas of the world. In the late 20th century, the Azores joined the European Union and became an independent province of Portugal.

Nowadays, the Azores are a popular tourist destination, and the islands have become known for their magnificent natural beauty and rich history. The archipelago is also home to a rich cultural scene, with traditional music and festivals being celebrated throughout the year.

Culture and tradition

The Azores, a group of nine volcanic islands located in the Atlantic Ocean off the coast of Portugal, has a culture and traditions that have been formed by its location and tumultuous past. The islands have been inhabited since early medieval times, and their culture is a mix of Portuguese, Spanish, and African influences.

The traditional cuisine of the Azores is based on local products and fish, such as tuna, swordfish, and sardines, as well as a range of vegetables grown throughout the archipelago. The most popular cuisine is the native stew, cozido das Furnas, which is prepared in a natural volcanic oven. Additional delicacies include carne de vinha d'alhos (meat marinated in wine, garlic, and spices) and bolo livedo (a sweet bread baked with sugar, yeast, and eggs).

The people of the Azores are normally quite warm and inviting to visitors. Music is an important part of the culture, with traditional fado songs being sung in bars and restaurants. The islands are also known for their festivals, especially the annual Azores Carnival, which takes place at the beginning of February and celebrates the start of Lent.

The islands of the Azores have a long history of fishing, and the art of making nets and baskets (cablecos) is still practiced today. The islands produce some of the best wines in the world, and local handicrafts, such as pottery, woodcarving, and basket weaving, are popular souvenirs.

The Azores are a beautiful and unique place to visit, and exploring the culture and traditions of the islands is an unforgettable experience. From the traditional cuisine to the music, handicrafts, and festivals, the culture of the Azores is sure to leave a lasting impression.

Religion

Religion is an essential aspect of the culture of the Azores, an archipelago located in the North Atlantic Ocean. The islands were invaded by Portugal in the 15th century, and the Portuguese brought with them the Catholic faith. Catholicism has been the predominant religion in the Azores ever since, though there has been a growing presence of other faiths in recent years.

The Catholic Church has a strong presence in the Azores. Nearly 70 percent of the population is Catholic, and the faith is practiced both publicly and privately. The islands have numerous churches and cathedrals, and the Catholic holidays of Lent, Easter, and Christmas are widely celebrated. The Catholic Church is also involved in public education, offering religious instruction and direction to students.

In recent years, the Azores has experienced a rise in various religious organizations such as Protestantism, Buddhism, and Islam. These religions have been increasingly popular, especially among the younger generations. Protestantism has been present in the Azores since the 19th century, and today there are various Protestant churches across the islands. Buddhism is a newer addition, with the first Buddhist temple opening in the late 1990s. Islam has also grown increasingly apparent in the Azores, with a mosque debuting in the capital city of Ponta Delgada in 2016.

Despite the presence of other faiths, Catholicism continues to be the main religion in the Azores. The Catholic Church remains a strong presence in the islands, and the faith continues to be practiced widely by the local population.

Climate

The Azores are a group of nine volcanic islands in the middle of the Atlantic Ocean that forms the Autonomous Region of the Azores, an autonomous region of Portugal. The climate of the Azores is subtropical and maritime, influenced by their location in the North Atlantic Ocean and its oceanic origin. The climate is moderate and humid, with typical temperatures ranging between 14 and 24 °C in summer (May-October), and between 8 and 17 °C in winter (November-April).

The Azores are very humid, with average annual precipitation ranging between 800 and 1,500 mm. The islands receive more precipitation during the winter months, when the northwest winds bring more rain and clouds, while the summer months are usually drier.

The Azores are also noted for their fierce winds, especially in the winter months. The wind is frequently strong and gusty, coming from either the north or the south. The islands are usually less impacted by the wind in the warmer months.

The Azores contain a broad range of scenery, from lush forests to cliffs and coastal meadows. The islands are also recognized for their remarkable volcanic activity, which can be observed in the various volcanoes, calderas, hot springs, and thermal lakes strewn throughout the archipelago.

In terms of vegetation, the Azores are home to a diverse range of plant types, from native plants to alien species from all over the world. The islands are also known for their unique and beautiful variety of wildflowers.

Overall, the climate of the Azores is mild and humid, with average temperatures ranging between 14 and 24 °C in summer and between 8 and 17 °C in winter. The islands are also known for their high winds, especially in the winter months, and for their diverse range of landscapes, from lush forests to rocky cliffs and coastal grasslands. The Azores are also home to a wide range of plant species, from native plants to exotic species from all over the world.

Population

The Azores is an archipelago of nine volcanic islands located in the North Atlantic Ocean, about 1,500 km (930 mi) west of Lisbon, Portugal, and roughly 2,800 kilometers (1,700 mi) from the east coast of North America. The Azores are considered an independent area of Portugal and are noted for their unique flora, wildlife, and terrain.

The population of the Azores is estimated to be around 250,000 people. The majority of the population is concentrated on the three most populous islands: São Miguel (158,000), Terceira (55,000), and Pico (13,000). The other islands have much smaller populations, with Faial having the fourth-largest population with 11,000 people and the remaining five islands having populations of less than 10,000.

The Azores is one of the most densely inhabited regions of Portugal and is home to several various ethnic groups. Most of the population is of Portuguese descent, however, there are also significant numbers of people with African, Brazilian, and Spanish ancestry.

The Azorean economy is largely based on agriculture, fishing, and tourism, and the population is largely centered around these industries. In recent years, the Azores has seen an increase in foreign investment, which has led to an increase in job opportunities and a corresponding increase in the population.

The Azores are known for their unique culture and friendly people, and the population is largely welcoming of tourists. The archipelago is also home to a multitude of various cultural activities and festivals making it a great trip.

Chapter 1. Basic Travel Tips

1. When to Visit the Azores

The Azores is an archipelago of nine islands located in the Atlantic Ocean, and it is recognized for its mild temperature. With its temperate temperatures and diversified scenery, the Azores is a superb year-round destination for vacationers of all kinds.

Spring (March-May)

Spring is a terrific season to visit the Azores, with temperatures ranging from mild to warm. This season is perfect for outdoor activities like hiking, biking, and swimming. The flowers are in full bloom, so it's a great time to enjoy nature walks. The days are longer, so you can make the most of your time on the islands.

Summer (June - August)

Summer is the busiest season in the Azores, with temperatures averaging between 70 and 85 degrees Fahrenheit. Now is the ideal time to visit the islands, as the weather is wonderful for outdoor activities like swimming, kayaking, and snorkeling. There are plenty of beaches to explore and plenty of festivals to attend.

Autumn (September - November)

Autumn is a great time to visit the Azores, as the weather is still warm, but not as hot as in summer. The temperatures range from the mid-60s to the mid-70s, and the days are shorter, so you can enjoy some peace. This is an ideal time to explore the countryside, go whale watching, and visit local festivals.

Winter (December - February)

Winter is a great time to visit the Azores, as the temperatures are mild and the days are shorter. This is the perfect time to go whale watching and explore the islands. It's also a great time to go hiking, as the weather is cool and the terrain is lush and green

2. How to go to the Azores

The Azores is an archipelago of nine volcanic islands located in the mid-Atlantic Ocean, roughly 1,400 km (870 mi) west of mainland Portugal. There are several transportation options available to get to the Azores.

By Air: The Azores are served by three airports located on the islands of Santa Maria, Terceira, and São Jorge. There are regular flights to the Azores from mainland Portugal as well as from other European destinations.

By Sea: Both passenger and cargo ferry services are operating between the mainland of Portugal and the Azores. The largest of these is the Santa Maria ferry, which sails between Lisbon and the island of Santa Maria.

Via Car: It is feasible to travel to the Azores from mainland Portugal through the island of Madeira. The trek is approximately 2,100 kilometers (1,300 mi) and takes around 36 hours.

By Train: Although there is no direct train service to the Azores, it is feasible to take a train from Lisbon to mainland Portugal and then take a ferry from there to the Azores.

By Bus: Regular bus services are operating between mainland Portugal and the island of Santa Maria. This travel takes roughly 16 hours.

By Cruise Ship: Several cruise lines offer voyages to the Azores. These usually depart from mainland Portugal and take around two weeks.

3. Best Time to Visit Azores

The Azores is a magnificent archipelago in the mid-Atlantic and one of the best-kept secrets of the Portuguese. With its nine islands and beautiful landscape, it is a paradise for nature lovers and adventure seekers alike.

The best time to visit the Azores is during the spring and summer months. The environment is moderate and sunny, with temperatures ranging from a mild 18 degrees Celsius in spring to a balmy 25 degrees Celsius in summer. It is the perfect time to explore the lush forests, rugged coastlines, and stunning beaches the Azores has to offer.

During the summer months, the Azores are the perfect destination for whale watching. The warm waters of the Atlantic are home to numerous species of whales, including sperm whales, pilot whales, beaked whales, and even the occasional blue whale. You can also spot a variety of dolphins, sea turtles, and other marine life.

The Azores are also a great destination for outdoor activities. Hiking, biking, and horseback riding are all popular activities, with many trails suitable for all levels of experience. You can also explore the island by boat or kayak.

The warmer months are also the perfect time to try native food. The Azores are noted for their fresh seafood, which is commonly paired with local fruit and vegetables. There are also lots of eateries serving traditional Portuguese cuisine.

No matter what time of year you visit, the Azores are sure to impress. With its distinctive geography, friendly locals, and breathtaking surroundings, the Azores will be sure to present you with an amazing holiday.

4. Things to do When you Arrive Azores

When you arrive in the Azores, there are numerous experiences to enjoy and things to do. Here are some of the greatest activities to do when visiting the Azores:

1. Enjoy the Natural Beauty: The Azores are known for their stunning natural beauty, consisting of lush green hills, rugged coastlines, and small towns. Spend some time touring the islands and enjoying their stunning scenery. Go for a hike to one of the many volcanic peaks and take in the view from the top. If you're feeling brave, consider canyoning or rock climbing.

2. Visit the Hot Springs: The Azores are home to several hot springs. Take a dip in the thermal waters and enjoy the natural therapeutic powers of the mineral-rich waters.

3. Eat the Local Cuisine: The Azores are known for their fresh and flavorful cuisine. Enjoy some of the native foods, such as cozido, a stew composed of pig, beef, and vegetables. Other local favorites include Azorean cheeses, as well as the famed Azorean pineapple.

4. Relax on the Beaches: The Azores are home to several stunning beaches. Enjoy a day relaxing on the sand and swimming in the crystal blue waves.

5. Go Whale Watching: The Azores are a great destination for whale watching. Take a boat excursion and observe some of the local animals, including sperm whales, pilot whales, and dolphins.

6. Explore the Towns: The Azores are home to some charming towns. Take a stroll through the cobblestone streets and discover the local stores and cafes.

7. Enjoy the Festivals: The Azores are known for their colorful festivals. From the Carnival to the Holy Spirit Festival, there are lots of opportunities to enjoy the local culture.

8. Go Surfing: With its world-class waves, the Azores are a great destination for surfers. Take your board and hit the surf.

These are just a handful of the activities that you can enjoy when you arrive in the Azores. With its spectacular natural beauty, great cuisine, and vibrant culture, the Azores are guaranteed to give a memorable experience.

5. Best Places to Stay in the Azores

1. Stay in a Guesthouse or Airbnb: The Azores is home to a wide variety of accommodations, including guesthouses, inns, and Airbnb. Guesthouses are a terrific choice for guests wishing to stay in the heart of the city, while Airbnb provides an intimate and unique experience. With many of the islands offering spectacular views of the Atlantic Ocean, staying in a guesthouse or Airbnb is a terrific way to soak in the natural beauty of the Azores.

2. Camping: For a more rugged experience, camping is a great option in the Azores. While there are no approved campgrounds on the islands, there are plenty of spots to pitch a tent or park an RV. The islands are home to spectacular landscapes, and camping is a terrific way to explore them.

3. Rent a Villa: For a luxurious stay in the Azores, renting a villa is a great option. Many of the villas provide spectacular views of the ocean, as well as modern amenities like private pools and hot tubs. The villas provide a terrific way to relax and appreciate the beauty of the Azores in elegance.

4. Stay in a Hotel: For travelers looking for a more traditional stay, there are plenty of hotels in the Azores. Whether you choose a tiny boutique hotel or a larger chain, there are plenty of options to fit the demands of each tourist. Hotels provide the convenience of being centrally positioned and close to facilities.

5. Stay in a Resort: For a truly luxurious experience, the Azores are home to several resorts. These resorts offer a variety of services, from spa treatments to gourmet dining. Many of the resorts also provide activities including golf, tennis, and horseback riding. Resorts give the perfect spot for a relaxed and elegant stay in the Azores.

Chapter 2: Travel Preparation

6. Entry Requirements

Entrance restrictions to the Azores vary depending on a traveler's nationality.

For most passengers, a valid passport is necessary for entry into the Azores. For passengers from certain countries, like the United States, a valid passport is not necessary. Nonetheless, tourists from these countries must have a valid visa or an approved ESTA (Electronic System for Travel Authorization).

For passengers from the European Union, a valid passport or national identity card is necessary. For travelers from non-EU countries, a valid passport and a valid visa are necessary.

In addition to the passport requirements, passengers must also produce proof of sufficient finances for the duration of their trip. The amount of monies required varies based on the length of stay, however, it is generally recommended to have at least €50 per day.

Visitors must also produce a valid return ticket, or documentation of further travel, to be accepted into the Azores.

Finally, travelers must present proof of medical insurance that is valid for the duration of the stay. The insurance should cover any medical expenses incurred in the Azores and must be valid for the entire duration of the stay.

It is important to note that the entry requirements for the Azores may vary depending on the traveler's nationality and the length of stay. It is always recommended to check with the relevant authorities for the most up-to-date information.

7. Types of Travelers visa

There are numerous sorts of Azores Traveler Visas that travelers may be qualified to apply for. They include:

1. Short-Term Schengen Visa: This type of visa allows travelers to stay in the Azores for up to 90 days for tourism or business purposes. This visa does not allow tourists to work or study in the Azores.

2. Long-Term Schengen Visa: This type of visa allows travelers to stay in the Azores for up to

90 days and can be used for either tourism or business purposes. With this visa, travelers are allowed to work or study in the Azores.

3. Transit Visa: This type of visa is required for travelers who are passing through the Azores to reach their final destination. It is valid for a maximum of five days and must be obtained before entering the Azores.

4. Tourist Visa: This type of visa is required for travelers who plan to stay in the Azores for a short period. It is valid for up to 90 days and must be obtained before entering the Azores.

5. Business Visa: This type of visa is required for travelers who plan to conduct business activities in the Azores. It is valid for up to 90 days and must be obtained before visiting the Azores.

6. Student Visa: This type of visa is required for travelers who plan to study in the Azores. It is valid for up to 90 days and must be obtained before visiting the Azores.

7. Residence Visa: This type of visa is required for travelers who plan to stay in the Azores for a longer period. It is valid for up to 90 days and must be obtained before visiting the Azores.

8. Work Visa: This type of visa is required for travelers who plan to work in the Azores. It is valid for up to 90 days and must be obtained before visiting the Azores.

9. Family Visa: This type of visa is required for travelers who are accompanying family members who are already living or working in the Azores. It is valid for up to 90 days and must be obtained before visiting the Azores.

8. Visa on arrival

The Azores is an autonomous area of Portugal, located in the eastern Atlantic Ocean, and is noted for its distinctive beauty, breathtaking scenery, and amazing wildlife. The Azores consists of nine islands, each of which provides something new for travelers to explore.

Owing to the increase in tourists to the Azores, the Portuguese government established a visa-on-arrival policy in 2019. This policy permits travelers to gain access to the Azores without having to apply for a visa in advance.

To qualify for a visa on arrival, visitors must hold a valid passport issued by a recognized country and show proof of sufficient funds to cover their stay and any other necessary expenses. Guests must additionally present documentation of a return flight and/or onward travel.

Visitors who are granted a visa on arrival to the Azores are allowed to stay for up to 90 days. During this period, visitors may travel freely between the nine islands. Unfortunately, travelers are not allowed to work or study while in the Azores.

A visa on arrival to the Azores is an excellent alternative for individuals who are short on time or want to stay in the Azores for longer than 90 days. However, it is vital to note that the visa on arrival is only valid for the Azores and cannot be used to gain admission to mainland Portugal.

In addition to the visa on arrival, travelers visiting the Azores may additionally need to secure a Schengen visa if they wish to go to mainland Europe. A Schengen visa can be requested at the Portuguese embassy or consulate in your home country.

9. What to pack

For Men:

-A pair of comfortable shoes: make sure to pack a pair of walking shoes, sneakers, or sandals that won't cause blisters or discomfort during your travels.

-Lightweight apparel: carry clothing that's lightweight and breathable, but also wrinkle-resistant. Adhere to light-colored textiles that won't absorb too much heat.

-A waterproof jacket: the Azores encounter some rain, especially during the cooler months, so make sure to bring a waterproof jacket or windbreaker just in case.

-Swimwear: if you plan on swimming or taking part in any water-related activities, make sure to pack a swimsuit or board shorts.

-Sun protection: carry a hat, sunglasses, and sunscreen to protect your skin from the sun's rays.

-A daypack: you'll need something to haul all your possessions about, so make sure to include a compact daypack or backpack.

For Women:

A pair of comfortable shoes: make sure to pack a pair of walking shoes, sneakers, or sandals that won't cause blisters or discomfort during your travels.

-Lightweight apparel: carry clothing that's lightweight and breathable, but also wrinkle-resistant. Adhere to light-colored textiles that won't absorb too much heat.

-A waterproof jacket: the Azores encounter some rain, especially during the cooler months, so make sure to bring a waterproof jacket or windbreaker just in case.

-Swimwear: if you plan on swimming or taking part in any water-related activities, make sure to pack a swimsuit or board shorts.

-Sun protection: carry a hat, sunglasses, and sunscreen to protect your skin from the sun's rays.

-A daypack: you'll need something to haul all your possessions about, so make sure to include a compact daypack or backpack.

-Comfortable dress: if you plan on attending any formal dinners or events, make sure to bring a comfortable dress or skirt that won't restrict your movement.

-Lightweight scarf: a lightweight scarf can double as a fashion accessory and a light layer to keep you warm in cooler temperatures.

For Children:
-Comfortable clothing: make sure to pack clothes that are comfortable and easy to move around in, such as shorts and t-shirts.

-Swimwear: if you plan on swimming or taking part in any water-related activities, make sure to pack swimsuits or board shorts.

-Sun protection: carry a hat, sunglasses, and sunscreen to protect your skin from the sun's rays.

-Sturdy shoes: pack a pair of sturdy shoes or sandals that will provide plenty of support and won't wear out too quickly.

-A daypack: you'll need something to haul all your possessions about, so make sure to include a compact daypack or backpack.

-A lightweight jacket: the Azores encounter some rain, especially during the cooler months, so make sure to bring a lightweight jacket or windbreaker just in case.

-Snacks: if your children are fussy eaters or need a fast snack on the road, make sure to include some of their favorite snacks.

Chapter 3: Transportation and Accommodation

10. Getting Around

The Azores is a group of islands in the North Atlantic Ocean, located roughly 850 miles (1,370 km) west of Lisbon, Portugal. This archipelago provides visitors with a wide selection of activities and gorgeous landscapes, making it a perfect destination for a vacation. But what's the greatest way to move around in the Azores?

There are different ways to move around in the Azores, including:

• **Vehicle hire:** Automobile rental is a popular alternative for travelers who want to explore the islands independently. Most of the major automobile rental firms have offices in larger towns, such as Ponta Delgada, Horta, and Angra do Heroismo. Driving in the Azores can be a bit tricky, since the roads are tiny and twisty, so visitors should be mindful to drive cautiously.

• **Bus:** There is an extensive bus network in the Azores, which covers all of the main islands. The buses are comfy and offer wonderful views of the landscape. However, the service might be unpredictable, so it's important to check timetables in advance.

• **Taxi:** Taxis are available in the major towns, including Ponta Delgada, Horta, and Angra do Heroismo. They are a good option for those who want a convenient method to go around the islands. Costs are modest, however, guests should always agree on a fare before getting into the taxi.

• **Boat:** Using a boat is one of the greatest ways to visit the islands of the Azores. There are regular ferry connections between the major islands, as well as boats that offer scenic cruises. Tourists can also charter private boats to explore the islands in more detail.

• **Air:** Tourists can also take use of the domestic airline network to see the islands of the Azores. The flights are usually moderately priced and give spectacular views of the islands from the air.

The islands provide a variety of activities, from historical monuments to magnificent landscapes, and there's something for everyone. So buy your tickets and get ready to discover the Azores!

11. Accommodations in the Azores

Hotels

The Azores is an archipelago of nine volcanic islands located in the North Atlantic Ocean, roughly 1,500 kilometers (930 mi) west of Lisbon, Portugal. With its mountainous landscapes, volcanic crater lakes, and abundance of natural beauty, the Azores is a popular destination for travelers seeking an escape from the hustle and bustle of city life.

With a diversity of housing options, from luxury five-star hotels to charming guesthouses, there is something to fit every budget and taste. Here are seven of the most popular hotels in the Azores:

1. Furnas Boutique Hotel & Spa: Located in the beautiful village of Furnas, this hotel offers stunning views of the crater lake and the surrounding mountains. Featuring modern rooms and suites, a spa, and an outdoor pool, this hotel provides guests with a genuinely unique experience.

2. Lagoa das Sete Cidades: Located in the town of Lagoa, this hotel offers stunning views of the twin crater lakes and the surrounding nature. It has modern, large rooms and suites, as well as a restaurant and bar.

3. Pousada do Monte Palace: This hotel is located in the town of Monte Palace and offers stunning views of the Atlantic Ocean and the surrounding mountains. Offering a choice of rooms and suites, it provides visitors with many amenities, including a pool and a spa.

4. Pousada do Castelo: Located in the old walled city of Angra do Heroísmo, this hotel offers stunning views of the harbor and the surrounding gardens. Offering a choice of rooms and suites, it also has a restaurant and bar.

5. Hotel do Caracol: Located in the small village of Caracol, this hotel offers beautiful views of the sea and the nearby island of São Jorge. With modern rooms and suites, it also features a restaurant and bar.

6. Pousada da Praia: Located in the town of Praia da Vitoria, this hotel offers stunning views of the ocean and the surrounding countryside. It has modern rooms and suites, as well as a restaurant and bar.

7. Pousada de Ponta Delgada: Located in the city of Ponta Delgada, this hotel offers modern rooms and suites, as well as a restaurant and bar. With stunning views of the harbor and the surrounding mountains, it is the perfect place to relax and enjoy the stunning natural beauty of the Azores.

Resorts

The Azores is a fantastic destination for individuals wanting a premium holiday experience. With its breathtaking landscapes, volcanic crater lakes, and abundance of natural beauty, the Azores has a selection of resorts to choose from. Here are seven of the most popular resorts in the Azores:

1. Lagoa Azul Resort: Located in the town of Lagoa Azul, this resort offers stunning views of the twin crater lakes and the surrounding nature. Offering a choice of rooms and suites, it also has a spa, a pool, and a range of activities.

2. Monte da Graça Resort: Located in the town of Monte da Graça, this resort offers stunning views of the Atlantic Ocean and the surrounding countryside. Offering a choice of rooms and suites, it also has a spa, a pool, and a range of activities.

3. Furnas Resort: Located in the town of Furnas, this resort offers stunning views of the crater lake and the surrounding mountains.

Offering a choice of rooms and suites, it also has a spa, a pool, and a range of activities.

4. São Miguel Park Resort: Located in the town of Ponta Delgada, this resort offers stunning views of the harbor and the surrounding countryside. Offering a choice of rooms and suites, it also has a spa, a pool, and a range of activities.

5. Horta da Paz Resort: Located in the town of Horta da Paz, this resort offers stunning views of the ocean and the surrounding nature. Offering a choice of rooms and suites, it also has a spa, a pool, and a range of activities.

6. Pico da Fonte da Areia Resort: Located in the town of Fonte da Areia, this resort offers stunning views of the ocean and the surrounding nature. Offering a choice of rooms and suites, it also has a spa, a pool, and a range of activities.

7. São Jorge Resort: Located in the town of Velas, this resort offers stunning views of the ocean and the surrounding nature. Offering a choice of rooms and suites, it also has a spa, a pool, and a range of activities.

Camping in Azores

The Azores is a fantastic destination for anyone wanting an outdoor experience. With its rough landscapes, volcanic crater lakes, and abundance of natural beauty, the Azores has a choice of camping alternatives to select from.

Here are seven of the most popular campsites in the Azores:

1. Camping Ponta Delgada: Located in the town of Ponta Delgada, this campsite offers stunning views of the harbor and the surrounding countryside. With a range of camping sites, it also features a restaurant, a bar, and a range of activities.

2. Camping São Miguel: Located in the town of São Miguel, this campsite offers stunning views of the Atlantic Ocean and the surrounding nature. Featuring a selection of camping sites, it also has a restaurant, a bar, and a range of activities.

3. Camping Lagoa: Located in the town of Lagoa, this campsite offers stunning views of the twin crater lakes and the surrounding nature. Featuring a selection of camping sites, it also has a restaurant, a bar, and a range of activities.

4. Camping Furnas: Located in the town of Furnas, this campsite offers stunning views of the crater lake and the surrounding mountains. Featuring a selection of camping sites, it also has a restaurant, a bar, and a range of activities.

5. Camping São Jorge: Located in the town of Velas, this campsite offers stunning views of the ocean and the surrounding nature. Featuring a selection of camping sites, it also has a restaurant, a bar, and a range of activities.

6. Camping Horta: Located in the town of Horta, this campsite offers stunning views of the ocean and the surrounding nature. Featuring a selection of camping sites, it also has a restaurant, a bar, and a range of activities.

7. Camping Vila Franca do Campo: Located in the town of Vila Franca do Campo, this campsite offers stunning views of the ocean and the surrounding nature. Featuring a selection of camping sites, it also has a restaurant, a bar, and a range of activities.

Guesthouses:

1. Sao Miguel Guesthouse: Located in Ponta Delgada, Sao Miguel Guesthouse is one of the most popular guest houses in the Azores. The guesthouse offers pleasant accommodations and services, including a swimming pool and terrace, a TV room, and a restaurant. Its ideal location is close to the city center and the airport, making it a wonderful choice for tourists looking for a comfortable and convenient stay.

2. Casa do Pico Guesthouse: Located in Pico, Casa do Pico Guesthouse is a great option for travelers looking for a relaxed and serene atmosphere. The hotel offers comfortable rooms, a swimming pool and terrace, a restaurant, and a private garden. It also has a terrific location close to the beach, making it a great alternative for beachgoers.

3. Vila Nova Guesthouse: Vila Nova Guesthouse is a popular guesthouse located in Sao Miguel. It includes spacious accommodations, a swimming pool and balcony, a garden, and a restaurant. The property is close to various attractions, including the city center and the airport, making it a convenient alternative for guests searching for a comfortable stay.

4. Villa Ana Guesthouse: Located in Ponta Delgada, Villa Ana Guesthouse is a great choice for travelers who want to experience the Azores in comfort and style. The guesthouse offers spacious accommodations, a swimming pool and balcony, and a restaurant. It also boasts an excellent location close to the city center and the airport, making it a convenient base for touring the Azores.

5. Casa da Vila Guesthouse: Casa da Vila Guesthouse is a popular and luxurious guesthouse located in the Azores. The hotel offers comfortable rooms, a swimming pool and terrace, a restaurant, and a private garden. Its position is close to the city center and the airport, making it a convenient alternative for those searching for a fantastic stay.

6. Casa da Vista Guesthouse: Located in Sao Miguel, Casa da Vista Guesthouse is a great choice for travelers who want to stay in a peaceful and comfortable atmosphere. The guesthouse offers spacious accommodations, a swimming pool and balcony, and a restaurant. It is also close to various attractions, giving it a great base for touring the Azores.

7. Casa do Monte Guesthouse: Located in Pico, Casa do Monte Guesthouse is a great choice for travelers looking for a luxurious stay. The facility offers spacious accommodations, a swimming pool and balcony, and a restaurant. It is also close to various attractions, giving it a great base for touring the Azores.

Rent a Villa :

1. Casa de Sao Miguel: Located in Sao Miguel, Casa de Sao Miguel is a popular villa for rent. The villa is equipped with a swimming pool and terrace, a garden, and a restaurant. Its ideal location is close to the city center and the airport, making it a wonderful choice for tourists looking for a comfortable and convenient stay.

2. Villa Marvao: Located in Ponta Delgada, Villa Marvao is a great option for travelers looking for a luxurious and comfortable stay. The home has a swimming pool and balcony, a restaurant, and a private garden. It is also close to various attractions, giving it a great base for touring the Azores.

3. Casa da Vila: Casa da Vila is a popular villa located in the Azores. The villa offers a swimming pool and balcony, a restaurant, and a private garden. Its ideal location is close to the city center and the airport, making it a wonderful choice for tourists looking for a comfortable and convenient stay.

4. Casa das Estrelas: Located in Pico, Casa das Estrelas is a luxurious villa for rent. The villa is outfitted with a swimming pool and balcony, a restaurant, and a private garden. It also has a terrific location close to the beach, making it a great alternative for beachgoers.

5. Casa do Mar: Located in Sao Miguel, Casa do Mar is a great choice for travelers looking for a peaceful and comfortable atmosphere. The home has a swimming pool and balcony, a restaurant, and a private garden. It is also close to various attractions, giving it a great base for touring the Azores.

6. Quinta do Canto: Quinta do Canto is a popular villa located in Ponta Delgada. The property is furnished with a swimming pool and terrace, a restaurant, and a private garden. Its ideal location is close to the city center and the airport, making it a wonderful choice for tourists looking for a comfortable and convenient stay.

7. Casa dos Ventos: Casa dos Ventos is a luxurious villa located in the Azores. The villa offers a swimming pool and balcony, a restaurant, and a private garden. It is also close to various attractions, giving it a great base for touring the Azores.

Airbnb:

1. Villa Canto: Located in Ponta Delgada, Villa Canto is a popular Airbnb for travelers looking for a luxurious stay. The property is provided with a swimming pool and terrace, a restaurant, and a private garden. Its ideal location is close to the city center and the airport, making it a wonderful choice for tourists looking for a comfortable and convenient stay.

2. Casa do Mar Azul: Located in Sao Miguel, Casa do Mar Azul is a great option for travelers looking for a peaceful and comfortable atmosphere. The property provides a swimming pool and terrace, a restaurant, and a private garden. It is also close to various attractions, giving it a great base for touring the Azores.

3. Quinta das Flores: Quinta das Flores is a popular Airbnb located in the Azores. The property offers a swimming pool and balcony, a restaurant, and a private garden. Its ideal location is close to the city center and the airport, making it a wonderful choice for tourists looking for a comfortable and convenient stay.

4. Villa Laranjeira: Located in Pico, Villa Laranjeira is a great choice for travelers looking for a luxurious stay. The property is provided with a swimming pool and terrace, a restaurant, and a private garden. It also has a terrific location close to the beach, making it a great alternative for beachgoers.

5. Casa da Vila: Casa da Vila is a popular Airbnb located in Ponta Delgada. The property provides a swimming pool and terrace, a restaurant, and a private garden. Its ideal location is close to the city center and the airport, making it a wonderful choice for tourists looking for a comfortable and convenient stay.

6. Casa do Monte: Located in Sao Miguel, Casa do Monte is a great choice for travelers looking for a peaceful and comfortable atmosphere. The property provides a swimming pool and terrace, a restaurant, and a private garden. It is also close to various attractions, giving it a great base for touring the Azores.

7. Villa Estrela: Villa Estrela is a luxurious Airbnb located in the Azores. The property is furnished with a

Chapter 4: Currency and Language

12. Azores currency

The Azores is an autonomous region of Portugal and its currency is the Euro. The Euro is the official currency of the European Union and is used by all 19 EU members.

The Euro is divisible into 100 cents, which is symbolized by the symbol "c". The Euro is issued in coins and banknotes. Coins come in denominations of 1 cent, 2 cents, 5 cents, 10 cents, 20 cents, 50 cents, €1, and €2. Banknotes exist in denominations of €5, €10, €20, €50, €100, €200, and €500.

The Azores is a popular tourist destination and many businesses accept Euro as payment. Credit cards, debit cards, and traveler's cheques are also routinely accepted. You can also convert your money to local currency at currency exchange agencies and banks.

When you are traveling to the Azores, it is vital to realize that rates may be different in different sections of the region. It is also vital to know the exchange rate between your currency and the Euro so that you can budget your vacation correctly.

The Euro is also used in other Portuguese-speaking nations like Angola and Cape Verde. In some of these nations, you may need to convert your currency into local currency before buying products and services.

The Azores is a beautiful place to visit and the currency you use can make a difference in your trip. Understanding the currency exchange rate and having some knowledge of the local currency might help you make educated decisions when you are traveling.

13. Where to Exchange Money in the Azores

The Azores is a beautiful and distinctive island of Portugal, located in the Atlantic Ocean. As a guest, you may need to convert money to cover your needs during your stay in the Azores.

One of the most popular and convenient places to exchange money in the Azores is at the **airport.** Your arrival airport in the Azores will likely have counters of currency exchange services. In the airport, you can exchange your country's currency for the Euro (the official currency of Azores) (the official currency of Azores). The currency rate at the airport is usually pretty fair.

Another option to exchange money in the Azores is at a **local bank**. There are several banks in the Azores offering currency exchange services, including BPI Azores, Banco Montepio, Novo Banco, and Caixa Geral de Depósitos. Each bank has its conversion rate and fees, thus it is advisable to compare the exchange rate and fees at multiple banks before exchanging your money.

Alongside banks, **several hotels** in the Azores also offer currency exchange services with competitive prices. So if you are staying at a hotel in the Azores, you can simply visit the reception desk to exchange your money.

You can also exchange money in post offices in the Azores. Most post offices have currency exchange services and the conversion rate is usually pretty good.

Finally, you can also find currency exchange services in some shopping malls, tourist spots, or souvenir shops in the Azores. However, it is recommended to double-check the exchange rate and fees with the shop before exchanging your money.

14. Money & Budgeting

The Azores is an archipelago of nine islands in the North Atlantic Ocean situated between Portugal and the United States. With its unique and beautiful natural setting, the Azores are a popular destination for travelers from both Europe and North America. The islands offer a wide choice of activities and experiences, from whale watching and sailing to hiking and understanding the local culture.

When it comes to money and budgeting for a trip to the Azores, the first thing to consider is the cost of airfare. Flights from the US and Europe to the Azores can be pricey, so it is crucial to investigate alternative possibilities and compare pricing. You can also look for discounts and package deals that include airfare, accommodation, and activities.

Accommodation in the Azores is also an important consideration. There are several options available, from luxury hotels to budget-friendly hostels and villas. Depending on your budget, you can opt to stay in a hotel, a hostel, or a self-catering villa. Be sure to research different accommodation options and compare prices to find the best deal.

Food and drinks can also be expensive in the Azores, so it is important to plan your meals. Eating out can be expensive, so consider packing your food or buying groceries from local markets. You can also save money by eating at local restaurants where you can try the local cuisine.

When it comes to activities, there are lots of possibilities in the Azores. There are plenty of beaches, trails, and water activities to explore. Many of the activities are free or inexpensive, so it is important to research before you go to find out what activities are available and what the costs are.

It is important to plan for transportation around the islands. Public transportation is accessible in the Azores, however, it can be restricted, so you may need to hire a car or take a cab.

15. Azores Language

The language of the Azores is Portuguese, a Romance language that is spoken by more than

260 million people around the world. Portuguese is the official language of Portugal, Brazil, Mozambique, Angola, Cape Verde, São Tomé and Príncipe, Guinea-Bissau, and East Timor. It is also one of the official languages of Macau.

The language of the Azores has been heavily influenced by the numerous other languages spoken in the region, most notably Spanish and English. This means that the Portuguese spoken in the Azores has a unique blend of vocabulary, phrases, and syntax that is distinct from other dialects of the language.

In addition to the regional dialect, the Azores is home to several minority languages, such as Faialese, a dialect of Portuguese spoken on the island of Faial, and Terceirense, a dialect of Portuguese spoken on the island of Terceira.

These languages are spoken by a tiny number of people and are in danger of becoming extinct, as the younger generations are progressively learning Portuguese as their first language.

The language of the Azores is a vibrant one, full of distinctive words, phrases, and idioms. That is a lovely example of how language may grow over time, as cultures come together and merge. As the number of tourists visiting the islands rises, more individuals are learning Portuguese and developing an interest in the language of the Azores.

16. Azores language phrases

The Azores is an archipelago of nine islands in the Atlantic Ocean which is part of Portugal and home to a separate language and culture. The

Azores language is a Portuguese dialect, however, there are many phrases and idioms peculiar to the islands. Visitors to the Azores should learn some of these words to help them converse more effectively with the natives.

These are 25 different Azores language phrases for visitors to use:

1. Olá (Hello): A frequent greeting used to say hello to someone.

2. Por favor (Please): A polite request for something.

3. Obrigado/a (Thank you): A nice method of showing gratitude.

4. Boa tarde (Good afternoon): A common greeting used when greeting someone in the afternoon.

5. Boa noite (Good night): A common greeting used when greeting someone in the evening.

6. Como vai? (How are you?): A polite way of asking someone how they are doing.

7. Sim (Yes): A positive response to a question or statement.

8. Não (No): A negative response to a question or statement.

9. Desculpe (Sorry): An apology for action or mistake.

10. Desculpe, eu não entendo (Sorry, I don't understand): An apology for not comprehending something.

11. Por favor, fale mais devagar (Please, speak more slowly): A polite appeal for someone to talk more slowly.

12. Não se preocupe (Don't worry): A phrase used to reassure someone.

13. Onde é o banheiro? (Where is the bathroom?): A courteous method of asking for directions.

14. Com licença (Excuse me): A polite way of asking for someone's attention.

15. Eu quero (I want): A way of expressing a desire for something.

16. Quanto custa? (How much does it cost?) : A polite manner of asking for the price of something.

17. Você fala inglês? (Do you speak English?): A courteous method of inquiring if someone speaks English.

18. Quando é o seu aniversário? (When is your birthday?): A courteous method of inquiring about someone's birthday.

19. Não faça isso (Don't do that): A way of expressing disapproval or warning someone not to do something.

20. Estou procurando o meu hotel (I'm looking for my hotel): A courteous method of asking for directions to a hotel.

21. Onde estou? (Where am I?): A courteous method of asking for directions.

22. Eu estou perdido (I'm lost): A polite way of expressing that one is lost.

23. Como posso chegar lá? (How can I get there?): A courteous method of asking for directions.

24. Pode me ajudar? (Can you help me?): A courteous manner of asking for aid.

25. Obrigado/a por sua ajuda (Thank you for your help): A polite manner of showing gratitude for someone's aid.

Chapter 5: Attraction and sightseeing

17. National Parks and Gardens:

1. Yosemite National Park: Yosemite National Park is located in California, USA, and is known for its towering waterfalls, lush meadows, granite cliffs, and giant sequoias. The park is home to more than 800 miles of hiking trails, over 3,000 species of plants, and several endangered species. It is a popular destination for campers, hikers, photographers, and nature lovers.

2. Grand Canyon National Park: Grand Canyon National Park in Arizona is one of the most popular national parks in the United States. The canyon is 277 miles long, up to 18 miles broad, and up to a mile deep. Tourists can take in breathtaking views from the South Rim, climb the canyon's many paths, and take a rafting excursion down the Colorado River.

3. Yellowstone National Park: Yellowstone National Park is located in Wyoming and Montana and is known for its geothermal features such as the Old Faithful geyser. The park is home to a broad assortment of animals, including bison, grizzly bears, wolves, and elk. Tourists can take in the breathtaking vistas of Yellowstone Lake, take a sightseeing trip, or go on a horseback ride through the park.

4. Great Smoky Mountains National Park: Great Smoky Mountains National Park is located in Tennessee and North Carolina and is the most visited national park in the United States. The park is known for its stunning views of the Appalachian Mountains, its rich biodiversity, and its many hiking trails. Visitors can explore the park by car, bike, foot, or horseback.

5. Acadia National Park: Acadia National Park is located in Maine and is known for its rocky coastlines, forests, and lakes. The park is home to over 120 miles of hiking trails, as well as historic sites such as the Bass Harbor Head Lighthouse. Tourists can take in spectacular views of the Atlantic Ocean, try kayaking or canoeing, or take a boat excursion.

6. Glacier National Park: Glacier National Park is located in Montana and is known for its stunning views of glaciers, mountains, and lakes. The park is home to a vast range of species, including grizzly bears, mountain goats, and wolves. Tourists can take in the views from the Going-to-the-Sun Road, go trekking or backpacking, or take a boat excursion.

18. Temples:

1. Angkor Wat: Angkor Wat is a temple complex in Cambodia and is the largest religious monument in the world. The temple was created in the 12th century and is an iconic emblem of Cambodia. Visitors can examine the complex carvings and sculptures, take in the stunning views of the surrounding environment, and learn about the history of the temple.

2. Prambanan Temple: Prambanan Temple is located in Central Java, Indonesia, and is one of the largest Hindu temples in the world. The temple was established in the 9th century and is notable for its stunning architecture and elaborate woodwork. Visitors can visit the temple complex, take in spectacular views of the surrounding terrain, and learn about the history of the temple.

3. Borobudur Temple: Borobudur Temple is located in Central Java, Indonesia, and is one of the most visited temples in the world. The temple was built in the 9th century and is known for its stunning architecture and intricate carvings. Visitors can visit the temple complex, take in spectacular views of the surrounding terrain, and learn about the history of the temple.

4. Wat Phra Kaew: Wat Phra Kaew is a temple complex in Bangkok, Thailand, and is one of the most important Buddhist temples in the world. The temple is recognized for its magnificent architecture and rich carvings. Visitors can visit the temple complex, take in spectacular views of the surrounding terrain, and learn about the history of the temple.

5. Kiyomizu-dera: Kiyomizu-Dera is a temple complex in Kyoto, Japan, and is one of the most visited temples in the country. The temple was erected in the 8th century and is notable for its beautiful architecture and elaborate embellishments. Visitors can visit the temple complex, take in spectacular views of the surrounding terrain, and learn about the history of the temple.

6. Meenakshi Temple: Meenakshi Temple is located in Madurai, India, and is one of the largest and most visited Hindu temples in the world. The temple was built in the 17th century and is known for its stunning architecture and intricate carvings. Visitors can visit the temple complex, take in spectacular views of the surrounding terrain, and learn about the history of the temple.

19. Islands:

1. São Miguel: São Miguel is the largest and most populated island in the Azores. The island is known for its stunning views of the Atlantic Ocean, its lush green landscape, and its thermal springs. Visitors can explore the many beaches, go whale watching, or take a tour of the volcanic crater lake.

2. Terceira: Terceira is the second largest island in the Azores and is known for its stunning views of the Atlantic Ocean, its vibrant culture, and its vineyards. Visitors can explore the many beaches, go horseback riding, or take a tour of the historic town of Angra do Heroísmo.

3. Faial: Faial is the third largest island in the Azores and is known for its stunning views of the Atlantic Ocean, its volcanic mountains, and its lush gardens. Visitors can explore the many beaches, go diving, or take a boat tour of the neighboring island of Pico.

4. Pico: Pico is the fourth largest island in the Azores and is known for its stunning views of the Atlantic Ocean, its volcanic landscape, and its vineyards. Visitors can explore the many beaches, go whale watching, or take a tour of the volcano.

5. São Jorge: São Jorge is the fifth largest island in the Azores and is known for its stunning views of the Atlantic Ocean, its lush green landscape, and its coves. Visitors can explore the many beaches, go kayaking or fishing, or take a tour of the historic city of Velas.

6. Flores: Flores is the sixth largest island in the Azores and is known for its stunning views of the Atlantic Ocean, its volcanic mountains, and its lush gardens. Tourists can explore the beautiful beaches, go hiking or bicycling or take a trip to the adjacent islands of Corvo and Faial.

7. Corvo: Corvo is the smallest island in the Azores and is known for its stunning views of the Atlantic Ocean, its lush green landscape, and its small villages. Tourists can explore the beautiful beaches, go bird watching, or take a trip to the adjacent island of Flores.

8. Graciosa: Graciosa is the second smallest island in the Azores and is known for its stunning views of the Atlantic Ocean, its volcanic landscape. Tourists can explore the beautiful beaches, go diving, or take a trip to the adjacent islands of Terceira and São Jorge.

9. Santa Maria: Santa Maria is the third smallest island in the Azores and is known for its stunning views of the Atlantic Ocean, its white sand beaches, and its lush gardens. Tourists can explore the beautiful beaches, go kayaking or fishing, or take a tour of the old town of Vila do Porto.

20. Beaches:

1. Praia da Vitoria Beach: Located in the municipality of Praia da Vitoria, this beach is surrounded by a stunning landscape that includes cliffs and a small harbor. It is a wonderful site for swimming, sunbathing, and visiting the local area.

2. Santa Barbara Beach: Located in the municipality of Angra do Heroismo, this beach is known for its crystal clear waters and white sand. It is a great spot for swimming, kayaking, and scuba diving.

3. Praia dos Moinhos: Located in the municipality of Lajes, this beach is surrounded by volcanic rocks and boasts crystal pure waters.

It is great for swimming, snorkeling, and exploring gorgeous surroundings.

4. Praia da Graciosa: Located in the municipality of Santa Cruz da Graciosa, this beach is surrounded by volcanic rocks and stunning cliffs. It is wonderful for swimming, sunbathing, and visiting the nearby area.

5. Praia do Porto Pim: Located in the municipality of Ponta Delgada, this beach is known for its crystal clear waters and white sand. It is a wonderful site for swimming, kayaking, and scuba diving.

21. Museums:

1. Azorean Museum: Located in Ponta Delgada, this museum is dedicated to the history and culture of the Azores. It contains a range of exhibits, including historical items, art, and traditional crafts.

2. Santa Cruz Cultural Center: Located in Santa Cruz da Graciosa, this museum is dedicated to the history and culture of Santa Cruz da Graciosa. It contains a range of exhibits, including historical items, art, and traditional crafts.

3. Angra do Heroísmo Cultural Center: Located in Angra do Heroismo, this museum is dedicated to the history and culture of Angra do Heroismo. It contains a range of exhibits, including historical items, art, and traditional crafts.

4. Lajes do Pico Cultural Center: Located in Lajes do Pico, this museum is dedicated to the history and culture of Lajes do Pico. It contains a range of exhibits, including historical items, art, and traditional crafts.

5. Horta Museum: Located in the municipality of Horta, this museum is dedicated to the history and culture of the Azores. It contains a range of exhibits, including historical items, art, and traditional crafts.

22. Palaces:

1. Palace of the Infante D. Henrique: Located in Angra do Heroismo, this palace was built in the 16th century and is one of the oldest buildings in the Azores. It is a UNESCO World Heritage Site

and contains a range of displays, including historical items and art.

2. Palace of the Capitães-Generais: Located in Ponta Delgada, this palace was originally built in the 17th century and is now a museum. It contains a range of exhibits, including historical items, art, and traditional crafts.

3. Palace of the Governors: Located in Horta, this palace was built in the 19th century and is now a museum. It contains a range of exhibits, including historical items, art, and traditional crafts.

23. Valley:

1. Furnas Valley: Located in the municipality of Furnas, this valley is known for its stunning landscape and hot springs. It is an excellent site for hiking, swimming, and exploring the local area.

2. Ribeira Grande Valley: Located in the municipality of Ribeira Grande, this valley is known for its lush vegetation and stunning views. It is an excellent site for hiking, swimming, and exploring the local area.

3. Sete Cidades Valley: Located in the municipality of Sete Cidades, this valley is known for its beautiful lakes and stunning views. It is an excellent site for hiking, swimming, and exploring the local area.

4. Pico Alto Valley: Located in the municipality of Pico Alto, this valley is known for its stunning scenery and lush vegetation. It is an excellent site for hiking, swimming, and exploring the local area.

5. Paul da Serra Valley: Located in the municipality of Paul da Serra, this valley is known for its stunning landscape and breathtaking views. It is an excellent site for hiking, swimming, and exploring the local area.

24. Churches:

1. Sé Cathedral of Angra do Heroísmo: This is one of the most important churches in the Azores and is located on the island of Terceira. It was built in the 16th century and is a combination of Gothic and Manueline styles. It contains a lovely main nave, a bell tower, and multiple altars.

2. Nossa Senhora dos Remédios Church: This church is located in the city of Horta, on Faial Island, and was built in 1799. It features a beautiful white facade with a bell tower and several side altars. It's one of the most important churches in the Azores.

3. Igreja Matriz de São Sebastião: Located in the city of Ponta Delgada, on São Miguel Island, this church was built in the 17th century. It has a Rococo facade, and a beautiful bell tower.

4. Igreja de São Pedro: Located in the city of Horta, on Faial Island, this church was built in the 18th century. It has a stunning Baroque facade with several side altars.

5. Igreja de Nossa Senhora dos Milagres: Located in the city of Ponta Delgada, on São

Miguel Island, this church was built in the 19th century. It's a Baroque-style church with a beautiful main nave, several side altars, and a bell tower.

25. Sea's:

1. The Atlantic Ocean: This is the largest sea that borders the Azores. It's home to a diversity of marine life and provides visitors with a unique experience.

2. The North Atlantic Ocean: This is the second-largest sea that borders the Azores. It's home to a diversity of marine life and provides visitors with a unique experience.

3. The South Atlantic Ocean: This is the third largest sea that borders the Azores. It's home to a diversity of marine life and provides visitors with a unique experience.

4. The North Atlantic Ocean: This is the fourth largest sea that borders the Azores. It's home to a diversity of marine life and provides visitors with a unique experience.

5. The Mediterranean Sea: This is the fifth largest sea that borders the Azores. It's home to a diversity of marine life and provides visitors with a unique experience.

6. The Indian Ocean: This is the sixth-largest sea that borders the Azores. It's home to a diversity of marine life and provides visitors with a unique experience.

Chapter 6: Activities in the Azores

26. Outdoor Adventures

1. Whale Watching: Azores is known as one of the best places to go whale watching in the world. The Azores archipelago offers some of the best possibilities to observe whales, dolphins, and other marine species. Besides the indigenous common dolphins, tourists can also view the largest mammal in the world, the blue whale.

2. Hiking: The Azores archipelago has some of the most beautiful hiking trails in the world. With its lush green woods, volcanic mountains, and breathtaking views of the sea, the Azores are great for exploring on foot. The trails vary in intensity, from moderate hikes to more tough routes.

3. Kayaking: Kayaking is a great way to explore the Azore's coastline and its many hidden coves and beaches. The tranquil seas make it a perfect exercise for individuals of all ages. The waters of the Azores are home to a variety of fish and other marine creatures, making it an excellent site to view animals as well.

4. Surfing: The Azores is home to some of the best surfing spots in Europe. The strong winds, huge waves, and empty beaches make it a perfect destination for surfers of all levels.

5. Swimming: The warm waters of the Azores are perfect for swimming. There are several beaches and coves to pick from, so it's easy to find a location to have a dip.

6. Mountain biking: The Azores archipelago offers some of the best mountain biking trails in the world. The routes range from basic to quite hard, so there's something for cyclists of all levels.

7. Climbing: With its rugged cliffs and volcanic mountains, the Azores is a great destination for rock climbing. There are several routes to choose from, so climbers of all levels can find something acceptable.

8. Diving: The rich marine life of the Azores makes it a great destination for diving. The warm, clear waters make it suitable for novices and experienced divers alike.

9. Fishing: Fishing is a popular activity in the Azores, especially for those looking for a more relaxed experience. The warm waters are home to a variety of fish, making it a fantastic place for both recreational and sport fishing.

10. Paragliding: Paragliding is a great way to take in the breathtaking views of the Azores. This is an activity ideal for people of all ages and experience levels, from beginners to seasoned pilots.

11. Horseback Riding: Horseback riding is a popular activity in the Azores, with many companies offering guided tours. The trails provide stunning views of the islands and the ocean, making it the perfect way to explore the Azores.

12. Canyoning: Canyoning is a popular activity in the Azores, with many companies offering guided tours. The canyons are full of natural beauty, and the experience of canyoning is both thrilling and gratifying.

27. Shopping

The Azores provides a range of shopping opportunities. From traditional open-air markets to high-end shopping in boutiques and malls, travelers can discover a choice of things to meet their needs. In the principal cities, like Ponta Delgada and Horta, travelers can find traditional souvenirs and local products.

For a more modern shopping experience, travelers can visit the shopping complexes in

Ponta Delgada and Horta, where they can find a great selection of worldwide brands.

Shopping Malls:

1. Açoreana Shopping Center: Located in Ponta Delgada, Açoreana Shopping Center is a popular shopping mall with a variety of shops and restaurants.

2. Forum São Miguel: Forum São Miguel is located in Ponta Delgada and is one of the largest malls in the Azores.

3. Madeira Shopping: Madeira Shopping is located in Ponta Delgada and is a popular shopping center with a variety of stores and restaurants.

4. Lagoa Shopping: Lagoa Shopping is located in Lagoa and is a popular shopping mall with a variety of stores and restaurants.

5. Praia Shopping: Praia Shopping is located in Praia and is a popular shopping mall with a variety of stores and restaurants.

6. Santa Cruz Shopping Center: Santa Cruz Shopping Center is located in Santa Cruz and is a popular shopping mall with a variety of stores and restaurants.

7. Angra Shopping: Angra Shopping is located in Angra do Heroismo and is a popular shopping mall with a variety of stores and restaurants.

Markets and Shops:

1. Mercado de São Roque: Mercado de São Roque is located in Ponta Delgada and is a popular market with a variety of stalls selling local produce, seafood, and handicrafts.

2. Mercado da Graça: Mercado da Graça is located in Ponta Delgada and is a popular market with a variety of stalls selling local produce, seafood, and handicrafts.

3. Mercado dos Lavradores: Mercado dos Lavradores is located in Ponta Delgada and is a popular market with a variety of stalls selling local produce, seafood, and handicrafts.

4. Mercado das Vendas: Mercado das Vendas is located in Ponta Delgada and is a popular market with a variety of stalls selling local produce, seafood, and handicrafts.

28. Local Crafts and Souvenirs :

1. Pottery: Pottery is a popular craft in the Azores, with many traditional pieces being handmade and sold in shops and markets.

2. Embroidery: Embroidery is a traditional craft in the Azores, with many traditional pieces being handmade and sold in shops and markets.

3. Lace: Lace is a popular craft in the Azores, with many traditional pieces being handmade and sold in shops and markets.

4. Woodwork: Woodwork is a popular craft in the Azores, with many traditional pieces being handmade and sold in shops and markets.

5. Wickerwork: Wickerwork is a popular craft in the Azores, with many traditional pieces being handmade and sold in shops and markets.

6. Leatherwork: Leatherwork is a popular craft in the Azores, with many traditional pieces being handmade and sold in shops and markets.

7. Basket Making: Basket making is a popular craft in the Azores, with many traditional pieces being handmade and sold in shops and markets.

8. Souvenir Items: Souvenir items such as t-shirts, keychains, and magnets are popular purchases in the Azores, and are available in many shops and markets.

Chapter 7: Events & Festivals in the Azores

29. Annual Events

1. Carnival of Ponta Delgada: This is a popular event in the Azores that takes place every year in February. It is a celebration of rich culture and customs that involve parades, dancing, music, and food. The festivities last for more than a week, and it is an opportunity for locals to have fun and show off their creativity. The festival culminates with the burning of the "Carnival King", a giant scarecrow-like figure that is torched in the middle of the city.

2. Festival of the Holy Spirit: This is an annual celebration that takes place throughout the Azores during May. It is a traditional religious occasion that is celebrated with tremendous grandeur. The celebration consists of a procession with a statue of the Holy Spirit carried through the streets, accompanied by music and singing. This event is a terrific way for locals to recognize their faith and bring the community together.

3. Azores Island Games: This is an international event that takes place every two years in the Azores and is open to athletes from all over the world. It is a multi-sport event that incorporates aquatic sports, athletics, basketball, and football, among other disciplines. This tournament is a terrific opportunity to visit the Azores' breathtaking environment and watch some of the world's greatest athletes compete.

4. Azores International Film Festival: This is an annual event that takes place each year in September. It is a terrific opportunity for filmmakers and cinema enthusiasts to come together and celebrate the art of film. The festival promotes the best of Azorean cinema and also incorporates films from around the world. The festival also includes panel discussions, workshops, and Q&A sessions with filmmakers and actors.

5. Azores Food Festival: This is a popular event that takes place throughout the Azores in October. It is a celebration of Azorean cuisine and comprises a variety of local dishes and specialties. The festival includes a variety of food vendors and restaurants, as well as live music and entertainment. It is a terrific opportunity to enjoy some of the greatest food in the Azores and discover the rich culture of the islands.

6. Azores Festival of the Sea: This annual event is held in the Azores in June and celebrates the region's maritime culture. The event comprises a range of events such as boat shows, marine exhibitions, concerts, and fishing competitions. The event also includes a variety of traditional folk dances, food stalls, and live music performances.

7. Azores International Marathon: This annual event is held in the Azores and consists of a marathon, half marathon, and 10K race. The event is held in May and is a great opportunity for runners of all levels to experience the Azores' stunning scenery. The event also includes a variety of activities such as post-race celebrations, live music, and food stalls.

30. Religious Celebrations

1. Easter: This is a religious celebration that takes place throughout the Azores during the springtime. It is a celebration of Jesus' resurrection and is marked by several traditional customs. On Easter Sunday, people gather in churches to pray and celebrate the resurrection. Afterward, families often gather for a festive meal and exchange eggs and chocolate.

2. Pentecost: This is a religious celebration that takes place throughout the Azores in May. It marks the descent of the Holy Spirit upon the Apostles and is celebrated with parades and festive meals. On Pentecost Sunday, people gather in churches to commemorate the event and pray.

3. Corpus Christi: This is a religious celebration that takes place in the Azores in June. It is a celebration of the Last Supper and is marked by several traditions. In Corpus Christi, people often congregate in churches to pray and celebrate the Eucharist. Thereafter, there are often processions with a figure of the Holy Sacrament carried through the streets.

4. Assumption of Mary: This is a religious celebration that takes place in August throughout the Azores. It symbolizes the ascension of the Virgin Mary into Heaven and is celebrated with processions and joyous dinners. On the day of the Assumption, people often gather in churches to commemorate the event and pray.

5. All Saints' Day: This is a religious celebration that takes place in November throughout the Azores. It is a celebration of the lives of all the saints and is marked by several traditional customs. On All Saints' Day, people generally assemble in churches to remember the event and pray. Afterward, there are often processions with a statue of the Virgin Mary carried through the streets.

6. Immaculate Conception: This is a religious celebration that takes place in December throughout the Azores. It is a celebration of the conception of the Virgin Mary and is marked by several traditions. On the day of the Immaculate Conception, people often gather in churches to commemorate the event and pray.

7. Christmas: This is a religious celebration that takes place throughout the Azores in December. It is a celebration of the birth of Jesus and is marked by various cultural practices. On Christmas, people gather in churches to celebrate the birth of Jesus and exchange gifts.

8. New Year's Eve: This is a religious celebration that takes place in the Azores in December. It symbolizes the end of the year and is celebrated with fireworks, music, and dancing. On New Year's Eve, people often congregate in churches to commemorate the event and pray for good luck in the next year.

31. National Holidays

1. New Year's Day: This is a national holiday that takes place on the 1st of January in the

Azores. It symbolizes the start of the new year and is celebrated with celebrations and fireworks.

2. Carnation Revolution Day: This is a national holiday that takes place on the 25th of April in the Azores. It honors the anniversary of the start of the Carnation Revolution, which abolished the dictatorship in Portugal in 1974.

3. Labour Day: This is a national holiday that takes place on the 1st of May in the Azores. It is a celebration of the labor movement and is celebrated by parades and demonstrations.

4. Portugal Day: This is a national holiday that takes place on the 10th of June in the Azores. It honors the anniversary of the death of Portugal's first king and is celebrated with parades and other events.

5. Azores Day: This is a national holiday that takes place on the 9th of July in the Azores. It honors the anniversary of the signing of the Autonomy Act, which granted autonomy to the Azores in 1976.

32. Restaurants

The Azores are renowned for their exquisite cuisine, and it is no wonder that the islands are home to some of the most celebrated restaurants in the world. From fine-dining places that serve traditional Portuguese delicacies to casual cafes that throw up the freshest seafood, there is something for everyone when it comes to dining in the Azores.

33. Traditional Food

1. Cozido das Furnas: Cozido das Furnas is a traditional stew dish of the Azores, cooked in the volcanic hot springs of Furnas. The stew comprises numerous slices of meat, such as pork, beef, and chicken, as well as potatoes, carrots, cabbage, and other vegetables. The unusual cooking procedure gives the stew a unique flavor and texture that can't be recreated anyplace else in the world.

2. Alcatra: Alcatra is a traditional stew dish that is made with beef, pork, or chicken. It is prepared in a clay pot and eaten with rice and potatoes. The stew is simmered gently over several hours to allow the spices to infiltrate and the meat to become soft.

3. Bolo Lêvedo: Bolo Lêvedo is a traditional sweet cake made of potato and wheat flour. The cake is scented with spices like cinnamon and cloves and is commonly served with sweet syrup or honey.

4. Sopa de Peixe: Sopa de Peixe is a traditional fish soup that is made with fresh fish, potatoes, and herbs. The soup is frequently served with a large loaf of bread and a glass of wine.

5. Carne de Porco à Alentejana: Carne de Porco à Alentejana is a traditional stew made with pork, clams, and potatoes. The stew is seasoned with garlic, bay leaves, and white wine.

6. Feijoada: Feijoada is a traditional dish made with black beans, pork, and beef. The stew is frequently served with rice and farofa, a traditional Brazilian side dish prepared with toasted cassava flour.

7. Açorda de Marisco: Açorda de Marisco is a traditional dish made with seafood and bread.

The soup is seasoned with garlic, coriander, and olive oil.

8. Espetada: Espetada is a traditional dish of grilled beef skewers. The beef is marinated in a blend of herbs, spices, and olive oil, and then cooked over a charcoal fire.

9. Sopa de São Jorge: Sopa de São Jorge is a traditional soup that is made with a variety of vegetables, such as carrots, potatoes, and cabbage. The soup is frequently served with a hard-boiled egg and a dab of sour cream.

10. Massa Sovada: Massa Sovada is a traditional sweet bread that is made with flour, eggs, sugar, and butter. The bread is commonly served with butter or honey and is a popular snack.

34. Street Food

1. Caldo Verde: Caldo Verde is a traditional soup that is made with potatoes, kale, and sausage. The soup is frequently served with a slice of bread and a dollop of olive oil.

2. Queijadas de São Jorge: Queijadas de São Jorge are small pastries made with cheese and eggs. They are frequently offered as an afternoon snack.

3. Salsichas: Salsichas are popular sausages that are grilled over a charcoal fire and served with a sweet and sour sauce.

4. Pasteis de Bacalhau: Pasteis de Bacalhau are small pastries filled with codfish and potatoes. The pastries are usually served as an appetizer.

5. Bolinho de Bacalhau: Bolinho de Bacalhau is a traditional dish of fried codfish croquettes. The croquettes are usually served with garlic sauce.

6. Carne de Porco Alentejana: Carne de Porco Alentejana is a popular dish of fried pork cubes that is served with garlic and white wine sauce.

7. Bolo de Mel: Bolo de Mel is a traditional honey cake that is served with a glass of red wine.

35. International Food

1. Italian: Italian food is popular in the Azores, with dishes such as pizza and pasta often served.

2. Chinese: Chinese food is also popular in the Azores, with dishes such as stir-fried noodles and dim sum often served.

3. Japanese: Japanese food is also popular in the Azores, with dishes such as sushi and tempura often served.

4. French: French food is also popular in the Azores, with dishes such as steak frites and croissants often served.

5. Indian: Indian food is also popular in the Azores, with dishes such as chicken tikka masala and naan often served.

6. Mexican: Mexican food is also popular in the Azores, with dishes such as tacos and burritos often served.

36. Seafood:

1. Mackerel: Mackerel is a popular fish in the Azores, with a mild flavor and oiliness that make it a delicious choice for grilling or baking. It is often served with garlic-infused olive oil, lemon juice, and parsley.

2. Octopus: Octopus is an iconic seafood of the Azores. It is traditionally cooked with garlic, olive oil, and sometimes potatoes. Octopus is commonly served with a side of boiled potatoes, boiled carrots, and tomato sauce.

3. Tuna: Tuna is a popular fish in the Azores, perfect for grilling or baking. It is frequently served with a side of boiled or roasted potatoes and grilled vegetables.

4. Shrimp: Shrimp is a popular seafood in the Azores, usually served with garlic and olive oil sauce. It is commonly served with boiled potatoes and cooked carrots.

5. Lobster: Lobster is a popular seafood in the Azores. It is commonly served with garlic, butter, and white wine sauce.

6. Clams: Clams are a popular seafood in the Azores, often served with a tomato and garlic sauce.

7. Mussels: Mussels are popular seafood in the Azores, typically served with garlic, olive oil, and white wine sauce.

37. Drink

The Azores are famed for their distinctive and tasty drinks, and there is no better place to experience some of the islands' delicacies than in one of the local pubs or restaurants. From the light and refreshing Vinho Verde to the sweet and aromatic Licor de Ginja, there is something for everyone to enjoy.

Vinho Verde is a light, pleasant white wine that is a favorite with locals and visitors alike. It is normally served chilled and pairs well with seafood meals. Licor de Ginja is a sweet cherry liqueur prepared using ginja berries, which are endemic to the Azores. The liqueur is served cold and can be savored on its own or as a digestif after a meal.

The Azores are also recognized for their unusual beers, and several local breweries manufacture a range of types. From light lagers to dark stouts, there is something to suit everyone's taste. In addition to beer, the Azores also produce several popular spirits. Ginjinha is a cherry liqueur, while Aguardente is a strong spirit made from sugar cane.

The Azores are also renowned for their coffee. Tourists may locate coffee shops around the islands, where they can sample some of the region's greatest blends.

38. Traditional Drinks:

1. Vinho Verde: Vinho Verde is a popular white wine in the Azores. It is light and crisp and commonly served with seafood dishes.

2. Licor Beirão: Licor Beirão is a Portuguese liqueur made with herbs and spices. It is traditionally served as an aperitif or digestif.

3. Vinho do Porto: Vinho do Porto is a fortified red wine from the Douro Valley in Portugal. It is a pleasant and mellow wine, great for drinking after dinner.

4. Ginjinha: Ginjinha is a Portuguese cherry liqueur made with cherries, sugar, and brandy. It is traditionally served in a short shot glass.

5. Aguardente de Medronho: Aguardente de Medronho is a Portuguese spirit made with medronho berries. It is traditionally served neat or with a mixer.

6. Cherry Brandy: Cherry brandy is a Portuguese liqueur made with cherries, sugar, and brandy. It is sweet and fruity and commonly served as an aperitif.

7. Moscatel de Setúbal: Moscatel de Setúbal is a Portuguese dessert wine made with Muscat grapes. It is sweet and fruity and excellent for sipping after dinner.

8. Madeira: Madeira is a Portuguese fortified wine made with a blend of grapes from the island of Madeira. It is commonly served as an aperitif or digestif.

9. Licor de Laranja: Licor de Laranja is a Portuguese liqueur made with oranges, sugar, and brandy. It is sweet and fruity and commonly served as an aperitif or digestif.

10. Aguardente de Medronho: Aguardente de Medronho is a Portuguese spirit made with medronho berries. It is traditionally served neat or with a mixer.

11. Poncha: Poncha is a popular local drink in the Azores. It is made with sugar cane rum, sugar, and lemon or lime juice.

12. Queimada: Queimada is a traditional Portuguese spirit made with aguardiente and flavored with herbs and spices. It is frequently served with a side of oranges.

Chapter 9: farming in Azores

39. Agriculture

The Azores is a small archipelago located in the middle of the Atlantic Ocean, midway between Europe and North America. Despite its small size and remote location, the Azores has a vibrant agricultural sector that is a major contributor to the region's economy. Agriculture has been a vital aspect of the Azorean economy since the islands were originally inhabited by the Portuguese in the 15th century.

The Azores has a warm climate and abundant rainfall, making it excellent for growing a wide variety of crops. The main agricultural products grown in the Azores are potatoes, sweet potatoes, maize, wheat, tomatoes, onions, beans, grapes, oranges, and other fruits. Livestock production is also important to the region's economy, with cows and pigs being the most common animals raised.

In recent years, the Azores has seen a resurgence of interest in local, sustainable agriculture. Small family farms have become increasingly popular, with many farmers focusing on organic and biodynamic farming methods. There has been a renewed focus on traditional varieties of crops and livestock, as well as an emphasis on preserving and promoting local food traditions.

The Azores is also a major producer of fish and shellfish. The waters around the islands are home to a variety of species, including tuna, sardines, mackerel, and bluefin tuna. Fishing has traditionally been an important element of the

Azorean economy, and many Azorean fishermen still practice traditional methods such as long-line fishing.

Agriculture has a vital role in the Azorean economy, and it is a major source of employment. Agriculture also contributes to the region's rich cultural legacy, with traditional farming practices, cuisines, and festivals all playing a part in local life. The Azores is an example of how a tiny location may make a huge effect on its economy through the development of high-quality agricultural products.

40. Fishing

The Azores are a unique archipelago of nine volcanic islands located in the middle of the Atlantic Ocean. The Azores are renowned for their great fishing grounds and surrounding waterways, which are plentiful with a broad range of fish species.

The Azores are home to some of the most productive fishing grounds in the world. These waters are filled with fish, including tuna, swordfish, marlin, grouper, snapper, cod, and mackerel. These fish are highly sought-after by both local and international commercial fishing fleets.

The Azores are also a popular destination for recreational fishing. The waters around the islands are famed for their great catches of many species, including tuna, marlin, swordfish, blue marlin, and more. The seas also house a variety of other fish species such as mackerel, barracuda, snapper, and grouper.

The Azores have a strong history of fishing and seafood production. The local fishing business has been a major source of employment for generations of Azoreans. Fishing is still an important source of income for many families and has contributed greatly to the economy of the Azores.

The Azores are also home to a wide diversity of traditional fishing methods and techniques. They include handlines, pots, and traps, as well as modern methods such as long lines, driftnets, and trawling.

The Azores are a paradise for fishing fans, with their breathtaking landscapes and plentiful marine life. Whether for business or leisure objectives, the Azores provide a unique and gratifying fishing experience.

41. Viticulture

Azores viticulture is the growing of grapes and the manufacture of wines in the Azores Islands, Portugal. The Azores is the only area in Europe where wine is grown in an archipelago, with the islands being home to some of the oldest vineyards in Europe.

Viticulture has been practiced in the Azores since the 15th century when the first people came to the islands. The Portuguese settlers brought with them the knowledge and practices of viticulture and began to plant grapes for wine production. Over the centuries, viticulture grew in the Azores and today the region is renowned for producing exceptional wines.

The Azores is blessed with a unique climate excellent for viticulture, with high temperatures and extended hours of sunlight. Its temperature, along with the volcanic soil of the islands, offers an environment that is perfectly suited to grape growth.

The Azores is home to various varieties of grapes which are planted for wine production, including Verdelho, Arinto, and Tinta Roriz. These varietals are used to produce the characteristic wines of the archipelago, such as the white Verdelho and the red Tinta Roriz.

In addition to wines, the Azores is also recognized for manufacturing fortified wines such as Madeira. This type of wine is made from fermented grapes and fortified with brandy, and is renowned for its distinctive flavor and aroma.

Today, Viticulture is an important part of the economy in the Azores, and the islands produce a wide range of wines for both domestic and international consumption. The Azores is also home to several wineries and wine festivals, which attract tourists from around the world.

The Azores is a beautiful and unique place to visit, and its wines are a perfect way to experience the culture and history of this archipelago. If you're seeking a genuinely unique wine experience, the Azores is worth a visit.

42. Forestry industry

The Azores are also home to a robust forestry industry, with a long tradition of sustainable forest management.

The Azores boasts a plethora of native forests, including coniferous and deciduous species. The islands are also home to a variety of non-native species, such as eucalyptus, which were imported in the 1950s. The forestry sector in the Azores is focused on sustainable management of the island's forests. This includes careful management of timber resources, the promotion of replanting, and the protection of fragile habitats.

The forestry sector in the Azores is based on two main activities: timber production and ecotourism. Timber production comprises the harvesting of trees, as well as the manufacturing of wood items such as furniture, construction materials, and firewood. Ecotourism includes activities such as guided hikes, bird watching, and educational programs.

The Azores' forestry industry has a long history of sustainable management, with an emphasis on protecting the islands' unique biodiversity. The government of the Azores has established several protected areas, including nature reserves, special conservation areas, and protected forests. The government also works closely with local landowners to ensure that logging is done sustainably.

In addition to timber production, the Azores' forestry industry also provides jobs to the local economy. For visitors, the Azores offers a plethora of options to explore its forests and enjoy its unique wildlife. Visitors can explore the islands' forests on foot, by car, or by boat, or they can join a guided trip with a competent guide. There are also various educational programs and activities offered to tourists, such as bird viewing trips and instructional classes.

The Azores' forestry business provides a unique opportunity to explore a beautiful and diverse region while learning about sustainable forest management. With its distinct ecosystems and magnificent landscapes, the Azores is a perfect location for travelers who are interested in learning more about sustainable forestry and the importance of conserving the environment.

43. Ways to Experience Azoreans Farming as a Tourist

Azores visitors can have an incredible farming experience during their vacation by taking advantage of the island's unique agricultural offerings. The archipelago, located in the middle of the Atlantic Ocean, is known for its lush volcanic terrain, temperate climate, and abundance of fertile land. Visitors can explore the many farms and gardens located throughout the islands and experience the unique terroir of the region.

1. Visit a Traditional Azorean Farm:

Visiting a traditional Azorean farm can be a great way to get a first-hand experience of Azorean farming. Azorean farms are typically small, family-run operations that focus on local and organic produce. Visit a local farm and take a tour to learn about the farming techniques used in the Azores. You can also sample traditional Azorean dishes prepared with the farm's fresh produce.

2. Attend a Festival:

The Azores are home to several local festivals that celebrate the region's farming traditions. Attend a festival to learn more about Azorean farming and sample traditional dishes made with freshly-harvested produce. You may even be able to participate in activities such as grape stomping or cheese making.

3. Participate in a Farm-to-Table Tour:

The Azores are home to several organizations that offer farm-to-table tours, which involve visiting a local farm and then eating a meal prepared with its freshly-harvested produce. You can learn about the different types of crops grown on the islands, such as bananas, pineapples, and papayas, as well as the traditional techniques used to cultivate them.

Touring a farm is a great way to gain an in-depth understanding of the local agricultural industry and to get an up-close look at the production process.

4. Take a Cooking Class:
Azorean cooking classes offer a unique opportunity to learn about the region's farming traditions. Take a cooking class to learn how to prepare traditional dishes using fresh ingredients from the Azores. These classes usually involve

visits to local farms and markets, so you can get an even closer look at Azorean farming.

5. Go Wine Tasting:

The Azores are home to several wineries that produce some of the best wines in the region. Take a tour of a local winery and sample some of the region's best wines. Many wineries also offer tours of their vineyards, so you can learn more about the process of growing grapes for wine.

6. Shop at Local Markets:

Azorean farmers often sell their produce at local markets. Visiting a local market is a great way to get a better understanding of Azorean farming. Here, you can sample some of the region's freshest produce, chat with local farmers, and even buy some of their products to take home.

7. Go for the volunteer program

If you're looking for more hands-on experience, you can also consider signing up for a volunteer program at one of the local farms. Many of the farms in the Azores offer volunteer programs that allow visitors to get involved in daily operations. You can work in the fields, help with harvesting, or even assist with the preparation of meals.

Volunteering on a farm is a great way to get a deeper understanding of the local culture and to gain an appreciation for the hard work that goes into producing the island's agricultural bounty.

Chapter 10: Entertainment in the Azores

44. Nightlife

The nightlife in the Azores is vibrant, with a choice of bars, clubs, and restaurants to pick from. The capital city of Ponta Delgada is the major center for nightlife in the Azores, having a large range of venues to choose from. There are plenty of bars and clubs that cater to all preferences, from energetic music venues to laid-back lounges. The Old Town neighborhood is particularly known for its many classic bars, pubs, and eateries.

For live music aficionados, Azores has a range of venues that present both local and international musicians. The Azores Blues and

Jazz Festival is held yearly in the capital and attracts some of the top acts in the blues and jazz worlds. For nightlife, Ponta Delgada has lots of alternatives, including some beautiful rooftop bars and clubs.

The Azores also boasts a wonderful range of restaurants and cafes, dishing up tasty local and foreign cuisine. Many of the restaurants are located within the Old Town, with plenty of outdoor dining and lovely views over the port. The surrounding islands of Flores, Corvo, and Santa Maria also provide a range of meals, including some great seafood places.

45. Bars and Clubs in the Azores

1. Casa da Cerveja: Located in Ponta Delgada, Casa da Cerveja is a popular bar and club in the

Azores. Boasting a wonderful range of beers, wines, and spirits, as well as live music and DJs, Casa da Cerveja is the perfect spot to enjoy an evening out with friends.

2. Corvo: Located in Ponta Delgada, Corvo is a lively bar and club. It boasts a great assortment of beers, spirits, and cocktails, and is recognized for its active nightlife.

3. Boca-Boca: Located in Horta, Boca-Boca is a popular bar and club in the Azores. With its trendy decor and pleasant ambiance, Boca-Boca is a fantastic location to meet and make new acquaintances.

4. Discoteca São Miguel: Discoteca São Miguel is a popular club located in Ponta Delgada. It offers a large selection of music and drinks and is known for its crazy celebrations.

5. Inferno: Located in Ponta Delgada, Inferno is an eclectic bar and club. It features a large selection of music and drinks and is noted for its energetic atmosphere.

6. Casa das Flores: Located in Ponta Delgada, Casa das Flores is a popular bar and club. It offers a large assortment of beers, wines, and spirits, as well as live music.

7. Café Gare: Café Gare is a popular bar and club located in Horta. It offers a large assortment of beers, wines, and spirits, and is noted for its colorful environment.

46. Live Music Venues

1. Casa das Flores: Casa das Flores is a popular live music venue in Ponta Delgada. It offers a wide variety of music styles, from jazz to rock, and features performances by local and worldwide acts.

2. Inferno: Located in Ponta Delgada, Inferno is a great live music venue. It provides a wide array of music types, from rock to folk, and showcases both local and international bands.

3. Corvo: Corvo is a popular live music venue in Ponta Delgada. It includes a wide array of music styles, from jazz to funk, and showcases both local and international acts.

4. Discoteca São Miguel: Discoteca São Miguel is a popular live music venue in Ponta Delgada. It showcases a wide variety of music types, from rock to salsa, and features both local and international bands.

5. Boca-Boca: Boca-Boca is a popular live music venue in Horta. It showcases a wide array of music styles, from jazz to blues, and features both local and international acts.

6. Café Gare: Café Gare is a popular live music venue in Horta. It presents a wide variety of music types, from rock to reggae, and showcases both local and international acts.

Chapter 11: Making Friends in Azores as a Tourist

47. Mingling with Azoreans as a Tourist

Azores is a beautiful archipelago in the mid-Atlantic, with a unique mix of cultures, landscapes, and activities. It is a terrific spot for travelers to discover and experience the culture of the Azorean people and their way of life. As a tourist, it can be intimidating to approach the locals, but there are certain tips and methods to make the encounter smoother and more pleasurable.

1. Respect the culture: Azoreans are very proud of their culture and heritage, so it is important to be respectful and mindful of this. Demonstrating an interest in the culture, traditions, and history of the Azores is a terrific approach to winning the favor of the people.

2. Be open-minded: The Azores is a diverse and vibrant place, so it is important to keep an open mind when it comes to the customs and traditions of the locals. Being open to trying new things and experiencing diverse cultures is a terrific approach to making a positive impression.

3. Learn a few words of Portuguese: Portuguese is the official language of the Azores, so learning some basic Portuguese phrases and words is a great way to start conversations with locals. That demonstrates that you are willing to learn about their culture and language and will make them feel respected.

4. Get involved in the local activities: The Azores is full of unique activities for tourists to take part in such as fishing, hiking, and exploring the islands. Taking up local activities is a terrific way to connect with the locals and get to know the culture and people of the Azores.

5. Visit the local restaurants and bars: The Azores is home to some of the most delicious and unique cuisine in the world. Visiting the local restaurants and pubs is a terrific opportunity to experience the culture and meet the locals.

6. Strike up conversations: Azoreans are friendly and welcoming people, so don't be afraid to strike up conversations with them. Ask them questions about their culture and lifestyle, and share your own experiences with them.

48. How to Approach Azoreans

1. Greet them warmly: Azoreans are very welcoming and friendly people, so it is important to greet them with a warm smile and a friendly hello. This is a terrific technique to make a strong first impression and start a conversation.

2. Be respectful: Respect is important when interacting with locals in any country. Take attention to local customs and etiquette, and be sure to address people nicely and respectfully.

3. Show an interest in their culture: Azoreans are proud of their culture and heritage, so showing an interest in their culture is a great way to approach them. Ask them questions about their culture and way of life, and offer your own experiences and knowledge.

4. Speak Portuguese: Learning some basic Portuguese is a great way to start conversations with locals. It demonstrates that you are interested in the culture and are prepared to learn about it.

5. Be friendly and open: Azoreans are very friendly and open people, so it is important to be friendly and open when approaching them. Be sure to smile, create eye contact, and be inviting when speaking with them.

6. Offer to help: Azoreans are very helpful and generous people, so offering to help out with anything they may need is a great way to make a positive impression. Whether it's helping to carry groceries or offering to lend a hand with a local project, this is a terrific way to get to know the locals.

Chapter 12: Day Trips from the Azores

49. Best Day Trip from Azores

The Azores is a group of nine volcanic islands in the Atlantic Ocean and is part of Portugal. It is recognized for its magnificent surroundings, lush green woods, and breathtaking beaches. The islands are a popular location for day vacations, offering a wide choice of activities and experiences. Here are some of the most popular day trips from the Azores:

1. Faial Island: This island is known for its stunning volcanic landscapes, spectacular whale-watching opportunities, and its charming harbors. Faial is home to the Caldera Volcano, which gives beautiful views of the neighboring islands. Tourists can also visit the northern coast of the island, which is home to some of the most magnificent beaches in the region.

2. Sao Miguel Island: This island is the largest of the Azores and is home to some of the most beautiful natural scenery in the region. In Sao Miguel, visitors can explore the lakes, springs, and hot springs of the island, as well as the spectacular crater lakes. There are also several hiking trails and bike routes to explore, as well as some of the best whale-watching possibilities in the vicinity.

3. Pico Island: This island is home to the highest mountain peak in Portugal, the Pico Volcano. Tourists can take the cable car up to the pinnacle of the volcano and enjoy amazing views of the surrounding. On the way up, travelers can stop at the Pico Wine Museum and sample some of the island's famous wines.

4. Santa Maria Island: This island is known for its stunning white-sand beaches and crystal clear waters. Guests can relax on the beach or take a boat excursion to discover the lush green trees and volcanic formations of the island. Santa Maria is also home to some of the top restaurants and pubs in the region, making it a perfect destination for foodies.

5. Terceira Island: This island is home to some of the oldest churches in the region, as well as stunning volcanic landscapes. Tourists may discover the island's history and culture, as well as its gorgeous beaches. Terceira is also home to some of the best seafood restaurants in the

Azores, making it a wonderful visit for seafood aficionados.

6. Flores Island: Flores Island is the westernmost of the Azores islands and is known for its stunning landscapes. This is a great place to go for a day trip, as there are several hiking trails, beautiful beaches, and some of the best bird-watching in the Azores.

7. Graciosa Island: Graciosa Island is a great place to visit for a day trip. This island is known for its stunning beaches, local wineries, and its traditional Portuguese villages.

8. Convo Island: Convo Island is a small, but beautiful, island located just off the coast of Faial Island. The island is known for its stunning coastal views and its picturesque villages. It is a great place to explore and relax, as the island is home to several great beaches and picturesque villages.

50. Best 7 days Azores Itineraries

Day 1: Arrive in Ponta Delgada

Start your 14-day Azores itinerary in the largest city in the archipelago, Ponta Delgada. On your first day, explore the city's cobblestone streets, charming cafes, and vibrant nightlife. Be sure to visit the São José Church and the 16th-century Fort of São Brás. Don't miss the iconic Igreja Matriz with its beautiful ceramic tiles.

Day 2: Visit the nearby island of São Miguel

On the second day, take a ferry to the nearby island of São Miguel, the largest and most populous of the Azores. Spend the day discovering the island's amazing natural splendor. Take a bath in the mineral-rich hot springs in Furnas, or explore the magnificent volcanic crater of Sete Cidades.

Day 3: Visit the old city of Angra Do Heroísmo

On the third day, drive to the old city of Angra Do Heroísmo, a UNESCO World Heritage Site. Spend the day visiting the city's cobblestone streets and Baroque-style structures. Don't miss the 16th-century São Sebastião Fortress.

Day 4: See the island of São Jorge

On the fourth day, take a ferry to the island of São Jorge. Visit the island's quaint communities and harsh terrain. Be sure to take a dip in the crystal-clear waters of the Caldeira de São Jorge.

Day 5: Visit the island of Pico

On the fifth day, head to the island of Pico, home to the highest peak in Portugal. Spend the day trekking the paths of Pico Mountain, or visit the vineyards of the island's wine district.

Day 6: See the island of Faial

On the sixth day, take a ferry to the island of Faial. Spend the day exploring the island's rough shoreline and volcanic environment. Don't miss the Horta Marina, the lovely harbor of Faial.

Day 7: Relax on the island of Terceira

On the seventh day, proceed to the island of Terceira. Spend the day lounging on the island's gorgeous beaches or touring its lovely villages. Don't miss the UNESCO World Heritage Site of Angra do Heroísmo.

Day 8: Visit the island of Flores

On the seventh day, take a ferry to the island of Flores. Spend the day exploring the island's magnificent landscapes. Don't miss the stunning views from the summit of Morro Alto.

Day 9: Relax on the island of Corvo

On the ninth day, head to the island of Corvo, the smallest of the Azores. Spend the day lounging on the island's lovely beaches or exploring its diverse surroundings.

Day 10: Visit the island of Graciosa

On the tenth day, take a ferry to the island of Graciosa. Spend the day exploring the island's charming villages and rugged coastline. Don't miss the breathtaking views from the top of the Mountain de Santa Bárbara.

Day 11: See the island of São Miguel

On the eleventh day, head back to the island of São Miguel. Spend the day discovering the island's amazing natural splendor. Don't miss the magnificent Lagoa das Sete Cidades.

Day 12: See the island of Saint Maria

On the twelfth day, take a ferry to the island of Santa Maria. Spend the day exploring the island's beautiful beaches and charming villages. Don't miss the iconic Vila do Porto.

Day 13: Explore the island of Faial

On the thirteenth day, head back to the island of Faial. Spend the day exploring the island's rugged coastline and unique volcanic landscape. Don't miss the lovely Horta Marina.

Day 14: Return to Ponta Delgada

On the fourteenth day, head back to Ponta Delgada. Spend the day exploring the city's cobblestone streets and vibrant nightlife. Don't miss the Igreja Matriz with its beautiful ceramic tiles.

At the end of this 14-day Azores trip, you will have explored some of the most spectacular and unique landscapes in Europe. From the lush natural splendor of São Miguel to the rough coastline of Faial, you will have experienced the finest of what the Azores have to offer.

Chapter 14: Safety & Security

51. Rules and Regulations in the Azores

1. Respect the Local Culture: Azores is known for their unique culture and traditions. Visitors should be mindful of the local culture, customs, and language. It is important to be courteous and respectful to the locals and to be mindful of local customs and traditions.

2. Respecting Nature: Visitors should be aware that the Azores is home to many unique and fragile ecosystems. They should respect the environment by avoiding activities that could damage the natural landscape, such as littering, off-roading, and camping in unauthorized areas.

3. Obey the Laws: Visitors to the Azores must obey all local laws and regulations. This includes traffic laws, such as wearing a seatbelt and respecting speed limits, as well as laws related to public behavior, such as no smoking in public areas.

4. Respect the Wildlife: Azores is home to many species of animals and plants, and visitors should not disturb the wildlife. Hunting and fishing are carefully restricted and tourists should only participate in activities that are allowed under the law.

5. Stay Healthy: Visitors should take measures to protect themselves from mosquito-borne illnesses, such as wearing mosquito repellent and avoiding outdoor activities during peak times.

Kids should also stay hydrated and use sunscreen, as the sun can be powerful.

6. Respect Private Property: Visitors should respect private property and refrain from trespassing or vandalizing private or public property.

7. Stay Safe: Azores is a generally safe destination, but visitors should take the usual safety precautions, such as not walking alone at night and not leaving valuables unattended.

8. Travel Responsibly: Visitors should be mindful of their impact on the local environment and economy. People should purchase local goods and services, and avoid behaviors that could affect the environment, such as damaging water supplies.

52. Security Measures in the Azores

1. Stay aware of your surroundings: Visitors should always be aware of their surroundings and keep an eye out for any suspicious activity.

2. Use a secure method of payment: When making purchases, visitors should use a secure method of payment, such as a credit card or a secure online payment service.

3. Keep your passport and other valuables secure: Visitors should keep their passports and other valuables, such as cash and jewelry, secure and out of sight.

4. Research before traveling: Visitors should research their destination before traveling, to ensure that they are familiar with local laws and customs, as well as any security precautions that should be taken.

5. Avoid walking alone at night: Visitors should avoid walking alone at night, particularly in unfamiliar areas.

6. Use caution when responding to requests for help: Visitors should be wary of requests for help from strangers and use caution when responding.

7. Be aware of your alcohol consumption: Visitors should be aware of their alcohol consumption, particularly if they are going out alone.

8. Report any suspicious activity: Visitors should report any suspicious activity to local authorities, such as police or security personnel.

53. Emergency Contacts

1. 112 – This is the emergency number for the Azores, to be used in case of any medical, police, or fire emergency.

2. Regional Health Service – The Regional Health Service operates a 24-hour hotline to provide medical advice and support in the event of an emergency.

3. Azores Coast Guard – The Azores Coast Guard is responsible for providing search and rescue services as well as responding to marine emergencies.

4. Azores Fire Service – The Azores Fire Service provides fire prevention, suppression, and rescue services in the event of an emergency.

5. Portuguese Red Cross – The Portuguese Red Cross operates a 24-hour hotline that provides medical advice and assistance in the event of an emergency.

6. Civil Protection Service – The Civil Protection Service is responsible for responding to natural disasters, such as earthquakes and volcanic eruptions.

7. Azores Police – The Azores Police are responsible for maintaining public safety and responding to criminal activity.

54. General Travel Tips

1. Be sure to check the local weather before traveling, as the weather in the Azores can be unpredictable.

2. Be aware of the local laws and customs, as they may differ from those of your home country.

3. Be aware of the local wildlife, as some species can be dangerous.

4. Be aware of the local environment, as some areas may be off-limits to visitors.

5. Be aware of your safety, as crime can occur in some areas.

6. When traveling around the islands, be sure to make use of the local transportation system.

7. Be aware of the local currency and its exchange rate, as it may differ from that of your home country.

8. Be aware of the local time zone, as it may differ from that of your home country.

9. Be sure to carry a valid passport and other essential documents when traveling.

10. Be sure to purchase good quality travel insurance before traveling, as it can provide peace of mind in the event of an emergency.

Printed in Great Britain
by Amazon

21386592R00112